VOCAL SELECTIONS – 2002 BROADWAY PRODUCTION

FLOWER DRUM SONG

ISBN 0-634-05510-0

WILLIAMSON MUSIC®
A RODGERS AND HAMMERSTEIN COMPANY
www.williamsonmusic.com
EXCLUSIVELY DISTRIBUTED BY

HAL•LEONARD® CORPORATION
7777 W. BLUEMOUND RD. P.O. BOX 13819 MILWAUKEE, WI 53213

Visit Hal Leonard Online at
www.halleonard.com

FLOWER DRUM SONG

YOU ARE BEAUTIFUL

Lyrics by OSCAR HAMMERSTEIN II

Music by RICHARD RODGERS

A HUNDRED MILLION MIRACLES

Lyrics by OSCAR HAMMERSTEIN II

Music by RICHARD RODGERS

Tranquillo *(calmly)*

dark blue cur-tain is pinned by the stars, Pinned by the stars to the sky, Ev - 'ry

flow'r and tree is a treat to see, The air is ver - y clean and dry. Then a

wind comes blow-ing the pins all a - way, Night is con-fused and up - set! The __

sky falls down like a clum-sy clown, The flow-ers and the trees get wet. Ver - y wet! A

hun-dred mil-lion mir-a-cles are happ-'ning ev-'ry

Coda (*slowly and tenderly*)

MEI LI: N.C.

day! _____ My fa-ther says the sun will keep ris-ing

o-ver the east-ern hill. My fa-ther says he does-n't know why but

OTHERS: It will! ____ Some-how or oth-er it will. ____

some-how or oth-er it will. _____

I ENJOY BEING A GIRL

Lyrics by OSCAR HAMMERSTEIN II

Music by RICHARD RODGERS

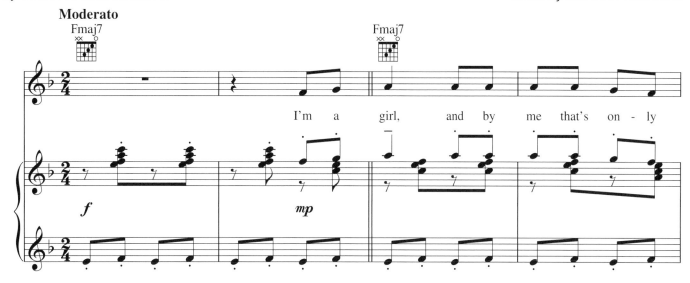

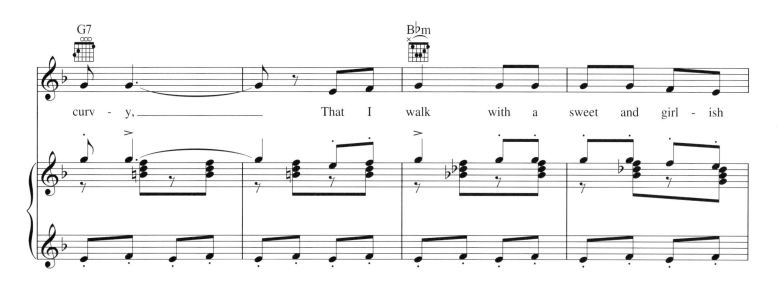

I AM GOING TO LIKE IT HERE

Lyrics by OSCAR HAMMERSTEIN II

Music by RICHARD RODGERS

where...   If he goes to an-oth-er place...   I am

go - ing to like it   there.

CHOP SUEY

Lyrics by OSCAR HAMMERSTEIN II

Music by RICHARD RODGERS

DON'T MARRY ME

Lyrics by OSCAR HAMMERSTEIN II

Music by RICHARD RODGERS

Refrain (Brightly)

(Sammy:) If you want to have a
(Mei Li:) (I would) like to see my

ros - y fu - ture_____ And be hap - py as a
sons and daugh - ters_____ Slid - ing up and down their

hon - ey bee,_____ With a hus - band who will
fa - ther's knee._____ (Sammy:) They'll have splin - ters in their

al - ways love you, Ba - by, Don't mar -
lit - tle fan - nies, Cook - ie, Don't mar -

44

Optional Ending with Coda

GRANT AVENUE

Lyrics by OSCAR HAMMERSTEIN II

Music by RICHARD RODGERS

Refrain

LOVE, LOOK AWAY

Lyrics by OSCAR HAMMERSTEIN II

Music by RICHARD RODGERS

FAN TAN FANNIE

Lyrics by OSCAR HAMMERSTEIN II

Music by RICHARD RODGERS

SUNDAY

Lyrics by OSCAR HAMMERSTEIN II

Music by RICHARD RODGERS

MY BEST LOVE

Lyrics by OSCAR HAMMERSTEIN II

Music by RICHARD RODGERS